Seul Choix, Our Home

Life at a remote Michigan Upper Peninsula lighthouse in the 1930s

Diane Reeder Elcoate, author-illustrator

For
Laurie

Diane Elcoate

National Library of Canada Cataloguing in Publication

Elcoate, Diane Reeder
    Seul Choix, our home / Diane Reeder Elcoate.
ISBN 1-4120-0685-6
    1. Seul Choix Lighthouse (Mich.)--History. I. Title.
VK1025.S42E43 2003   386'.855'0922774935   C2003-903830-0

TRAFFORD

This book was published *on-demand* in cooperation with Trafford Publishing.
On-demand publishing is a unique process and service of making a book available for retail sale to the public taking advantage of on-demand manufacturing and Internet marketing. **On-demand publishing** includes promotions, retail sales, manufacturing, order fulfilment, accounting and collecting royalties on behalf of the author.

Suite 6E, 2333 Government St., Victoria, B.C. V8T 4P4, CANADA

Phone	250-383-6864	Toll-free 1-888-232-4444 (Canada & US)	
Fax	250-383-6804	E-mail sales@trafford.com	
Web site	www.trafford.com	TRAFFORD PUBLISHING IS A DIVISION OF TRAFFORD HOLDINGS LTD.	
Trafford Catalogue #03-1055		www.trafford.com/robots/03-1055.html	

10   9   8   7   6   5   4   3   2

LAKE SUPERIOR

MICHIGAN

Upper Penins

Seul
Choix Point

Beaver Island

LAKE MICHIGAN

CANADA

Sault Saint Marie

ula

Mackinac Island

Straits of Mackinac

LAKE

HURON

MICHIGAN

Lower Peninsula

Seul Choix, Our Home

Margaret opened one eye and looked around her old, familiar room. Late summer sun shone in through the open window. Waves lapped gently at the rocks just outside the house. She was lying on her mattress on the floor. Cleo was curled up next to her. She opened both eyes and sat up quickly. From the other room she could hear her mother talking to John, the tug boat captain. He had helped her father and brother, Thomas, load most of their belongings on to the barge last night. Now, she remembered. This was moving day!

A mosquito buzzed near her face and she swatted at it. She found the clothes she had taken off last night. Quickly, she pulled on the faded overalls, some that Thomas had outgrown, and buttoned up her old pink blouse before going into the kitchen. Cleo, her cat, yawned and stretched and followed Margaret out of the room.

Margaret was eight and this lighthouse on the south end of Beaver Island was the only home she could remember. Her father was the keeper here but recently he had been given orders to go to Seul Choix Point on the mainland of Michigan's Upper Peninsula to become assistant keeper there.

"Is it time to go?", Margaret asked her mother who was standing at the old cook stove, dishing up oatmeal.

"Almost", her mother answered, "But first, you need to eat some breakfast. This will be a long, busy day," said Mother as she handed Margaret the dish of oatmeal with evaporated milk. Margaret took it and a spoon and headed for the porch steps. Cleo followed. As Margaret ate her breakfast, she watched her older brother, Thomas, and John load some more crates and pieces of furniture. And finally, her mother's brand new washing machine was loaded and tied securely with rope. She set her half-eaten dish of oatmeal down for Cleo to finish. She was much too excited for food, right now.

She had never known any other home than this lighthouse on Beaver Island. She had been born here. An old midwife from the village had come to the lighthouse, to help her mother the night Margaret was born. Margaret grew up on the beach and in the fields behind the lighthouse, playing with Cleo and her dolls. But today the family would move to another lighthouse. They were about to board a tug that would take them through the islands north of Beaver Island and across this big lake that looked like an ocean.

"Margaret, bring Cleo down here and put her in this crate," John, the tugboat captain, called to her from the dock. "It's time to leave." John watched as Margaret stuffed the reluctant cat into the crate, unhooking her claws from the edges. Gently, he put the lid on and tied it down, making a rope handle at the top.

"I think it would be best if we all squeezed into the cabin," Father said.

Thomas put Cleo's cage on top of the pile of goods on the barge and tied it to one of the ropes holding the furniture in place. Then he helped his mother and sister up into the tug boat. Thomas and his father threw off the ropes that tied the barge to the dock and then jumped up to join the tug captain and the rest of the family in the small cabin. The tug began to first push and then to pull the barge away from the dock and away from the island.

They passed St. James Harbor and could see the village where Margaret had sometimes gone with her mother to shop. There were many large and small ships tied at the docks in the harbor. The tug rounded the point and passed near Garden Island and some smaller islands before heading west out into the open water of Lake Michigan.

Margaret sat quietly next to her mother and watched behind them, as the islands grew dimmer and then turned into dark bumps on the horizon. Suddenly she realized that she couldn't see any land in front or behind them.

At first the water was calm and smooth and they made good time but as they moved further out into open water, gentle swells gave way to huge choppy waves with deep troughs. The barge and tug began to rock until Margaret felt dizzy and sick.

Mother wrapped the big shawl tighter around both of them. Cleo began to yowl in her cage out on the barge. Mother was uneasy but Margaret was frightened. She looked at her mother's face but saw no signs of fear so she stayed calm in spite of feeling fearful and seasick.

"We'll soon be out of this and into the shelter of Seul Choix," John told them.

"Strong winds near Chicago churned up the length of Lake Michigan yesterday and now those waves are just reaching the north shore," Thomas explained with his fourteen-year-old wisdom. He had learned that from his father and from John, who were both seasoned sailors on the Great Lakes.

"Father explained to me how this place we're going to got it's name," Thomas continued. "More than two hundred years ago French fur traders trapped beaver in the streams and smaller lakes near Lake Michigan, during the winters. After the ice broke up in the spring, they piled their dried pelts in their dugout canoes and took them to the fur markets on Mackinac Island, sixty miles east of Seul Choix. The Astor Fur Market was the largest one and I think it's still there. Those rich folks in New York City and Paris and London sure love to wear hats and coats made of fur, and those fur-bearing animals live right here."

"The fur traders were called "Voyagers" and they paddled their canoes piled high with pelts and followed the shoreline, then crossed the Straits of Mackinac to Mackinaw Island to the markets. They were happy-go-lucky men who sang and joked as they paddled along. They're the ones who named the harbor Seul Choix. That means "only choice," in French. Unless you speak French, it's hard to know how to spell it when you hear it pronounced "sis-shwa." It looks like something else. It is a safe harbor."

"There are many French names in the Great Lakes area because of all the French explorers," continued Thomas. "Some of those names are, the Straits of Mackinac where Lake Michigan, Lake Huron and Lake Superior join each other through the rapids and canal at Sault Saint Marie. There were locks built there in 1855 so that large ships can go through the rapids to and from Lake Superior to factories down near Chicago. They carry iron ore from Duluth, Minnesota, and Marquette, Michigan, to make into steel in the mills near Chicago. There was even a war fought by the French and English in the 1700's because the Straits area was so important to world trade. Did you know that all of the Great Lakes are connected to the Atlantic Ocean through the Saint Lawrence River, through Canada? How's that for a geography and history lesson?"

John spoke up. "Thomas, you should become a teacher. You know so much about so many things, already and you're interested in everything."

Just then waves began to wash over the barge and splatter on to the windows of the tug.

"Oh, no," Margaret heard her mother cry as she looked back at the barge.

Margaret stood on tiptoes to see what her mother saw. The washing machine, that new Maytag washing machine that her mother was so proud of, had somehow broken free of its ropes and was slowly inching toward the edge of the barge. The next big wave toppled it into a watery grave.

"I waited so long for that and now it's gone," she said quietly, with her hands over her face.

At least it wasn't Cleo, Margaret thought as she looked to see her wet cat, pacing in the crate but still tied on.

Just as quickly as the waves had come, they quieted and now Margaret could see a point of land emerging from the water and landscape. As they came nearer, thick cedar trees covered the point but she could make out a clearing where a white light tower was connected to a red roof, held up by a big, brick house with white gables.

It looks like a castle in a storybook, thought Margaret.

"Your new home," announced John. "We're here! I'm really sorry about losing your washing machine overboard, Ma'am", he apologized.

"I'm sad, too," mother replied, "But we all got here safely." She looked out at the barge and at her husband and son, now standing next to the pile of household goods still anchored down with rope.

Before long, the barge was secured to the dock at Seul Choix. Captain Rogers and two lighthouse assistants had come down to the tug to greet the new arrivals and to help unload the barge.

"That was some wild ride," Thomas yelled as he jumped off the barge and down on the dock.

Captain Rogers helped Margaret jump down to the dock. "Welcome to you, young lady."

"Hello", said Margaret, shyly.

Thomas untied Cleo's cage and handed it to Margaret. Cleo was wet and wild-eyed, but seemed to be all right, otherwise. Margaret reached her fingers in to stroke Cleo's nose.

Everyone was introduced. Mrs. Rogers put her arm around Margaret's shoulders. "Welcome to Seul Choix, your new home."

When Margaret looked up at Mrs. Rogers, she noticed the white gable ends of the house that bowed like the sides of a ship. Someone had given lots of thought and time to design such a symbolic place, way out here in the wilderness.

I'm going to like it here, thought Margaret.

Margaret picked up Cleo in her cage and with her mother, followed Mrs. Rogers up to the house. They went across a long porch and into the front door. Mrs. Rogers knocked lightly at an inside door and then pushed it open. They were in the office and a young Coast Guardsman sat behind the desk writing in a large open ledger.

"Hello, Owen," said Mrs. Rogers. "This is Margaret and her mother. They just arrived from Beaver Island. The barge with their household goods is being unloaded now."

"Nice to meet you, ma'am and Margaret. Excuse me, I'm recording the tug and barge that brought you here. Keeping the logs accurately is required by the government offices. But, later on I'll be happy to show you around. Would you like to climb the steps and inspect our third order Fresnel lens? We're real proud of that light. It can be seen by ships at least seventeen miles away. That keeps us busy cleaning and fueling. It's a beauty!"

We'll be back later," Mrs. Rogers called to Owen as she led Margaret and her mother back toward the porch steps and to their doorway. She opened the door to their kitchen and Margaret and Mother followed her into a light, spacious kitchen, just waiting for the new family's possessions. Through the kitchen door was a hallway which led to the stairway and the second floor. She set Cleo's cage on the floor next to the door.

"About ten years ago, before you were born, Margaret, this wall--she put her right hand on a plastered wall next to the stairs--was put here to divide the house into a duplex for two families. Mr. Rogers and I live on the other side. Come on upstairs and I'll show you the rest of your house." At the top of the stairs, Margaret could see three big bedrooms.

"Which room would you like?" asked her mother.

"I think this would be good for my room," Margaret said, walking into the room on the right, at the end of the short hall.

"Look, I even have my own closet! Thomas can have that one and you and Papa need to take the front room. You can see the harbor from there."

"You can also see the light in the lighthouse," explained Mrs. Rogers. "Come over here to the window and look up. Do you see that round mirror attached to the gable? You could see yourself if you stood in the right place."

That's a funny place for a mirror, thought Margaret but when she looked, she could see the top of the lighthouse reflected in the mirror.

"This room has been set up for the light keeper, so he can keep track of the light at night without going outside or up to the top of the tower. So, this is where your parents need to be, Margaret," explained Mrs. Rogers.

By now she could hear her father's voice downstairs. He and Thomas and some others were already bringing in the furniture and crates from the barge. When Margaret and her mother and Mrs. Rogers went back downstairs, they had to squeeze past crates and pieces of furniture piled in the hallway.

"Margaret, why don't you and your mother come with me to our side of the house while the men get your things set up?"

Margaret and her mother followed Mrs. Rogers to another doorway that led into her big, comfortable kitchen and eating area. Delicious smells of chicken stew and biscuits filled the air.

"Please sit at the table while I get you something to eat."

Mrs. Rogers was used to cooking for lots of people.

"Besides my husband and yours, there are two assistants who sleep in the loft over the horse stables. You met one of them, Owen, you remember. They take their meals here and there are often inspectors and others who come off the ships and have business at the lighthouse. Sometimes some have to wait out a storm before they can go back out on the lake. That's when my chicken coop and big garden come in handy. I'm a pretty good shot during deer season, too."

Margaret wasn't very hungry. The events of moving day and being in a strange place had stolen her appetite. The broth from the stew tasted good and she ate half a biscuit spread thickly with blackberry jam.

Captain Rogers popped his head in the doorway.

"Margaret, your room is all ready for you."

It's been a long, tiring day, Margaret," Mother said. "Come along up to your new room. Cleo is waiting for you. I'll help you get ready and then we'll read the next chapter in your book, THE BOBBSEY TWINS AT SNOWFLAKE LODGE. We want to finish before the supply ship comes again. It's due next week."

Even though Margaret could read, she liked this time that she spent alone with her mother. As Mama read, near the end of the book where the twins were listening to the story of Mr. Carfor's life, Margaret began to feel very sleepy. Cleo was curled up next to her, warm and purring. Mama closed the book and laid it on a chair beside the bed. She kissed her daughter's forehead and went downstairs. There was still so much to unpack and organize before she would be ready to fix breakfast for her family in the morning.

Margaret slept so late the next morning that her mother had to awaken her. She was dreaming and was back on Beaver Island, playing on the beach with her friend Mary, when she realized that her mother was calling her from the stairway in their new home.

"I'm up", Margaret called down to her mother. She jumped out of her familiar bed into an unfamiliar room and put on the same rumpled clothes that she'd worn yesterday for the trip here. She followed the stairway down to the kitchen and found her mother dishing up the last of the oatmeal for her.

"Good morning, Sweetheart. How are you feeling today? I guess you slept well."

"Good morning, Mama", Margaret responded. "Yes. I slept like Cleo does and I feel good."

Margaret poured evaporated milk from the pitcher on to her bowl of oatmeal.

"I'm really hungry today." She proved it by eating every bit of her breakfast. Cleo sat beside her chair, looking up at her and hoping to finish Margaret's oatmeal again but she was disappointed this time.

Thomas came bounding into the kitchen. "Hurry up, Margaret. I want to show you around the place." They went outside and could see the dock. It was empty. The tug and barge had gone back to Beaver Island.

"Look here." Thomas pointed to the large brick building in the yard, down toward the opposite shore of the point. "That's the Fog Signal Building. One of the assistants has promised to let me help him next time he has to fire up the steam engine to run the horns. Come around here, toward the lake. See those two big horns sticking out of the gable up by the roof? They must be really loud! I can hardly wait!"

Thomas led the way inside the building to show his sister the big steam compressor. "It takes almost half an hour after the fire is going in the boiler to make enough steam to get everything running," Thomas explained.

Today was a perfect summer day and Margaret couldn't imagine that fog would be a problem anytime, soon. Her brother went on ahead of her and climbed the spiral stairway to the loft where pipes connected to the foghorns poked through the wall. "I can hardly wait," he said again to himself.

Margaret was outside in the yard when Thomas came back down the stairs. The screen door banged behind him as he walked toward her.

"Those are paint and fuel storage buildings," Thomas explained as he pointed to the two narrow brick buildings that looked like privies. "That stuff is highly explosive and can't be stored near anything else." Margaret could see padlocks on the doors and so she knew that they were dangerous places that only certain people were allowed to enter.

"These storage buildings are much stronger than the sheds we had on Beaver Island," Thomas said.

Margaret turned around to look up at the tall, white, light tower. One of the assistants was dangling from a rope seat, giving the brick tower a new coat of paint. Another man was below him, scraping loose paint from the bricks, preparing for the new coat of paint.

"This is a job we have to do every summer," the painter called down to Margaret and her brother. "Winter storms are rough on buildings out here on the point."

Margaret tipped her head back and squinted her eyes to look at the full length of the tower. "There are windows in this tower," she exclaimed.

"Yes", replied Thomas, "And there's a long spiral stairway that goes all the way to the top," pointing to the windows of the glass enclosure nearly eighty feet up. "I'll take you up to see the light when one of the men is free to go with us. We're not allowed to go up without an escort, yet."

Mrs. Rogers called from her porch, "Would you like to help me make cookies, Margaret?"

"Oh, yes. That will be fun!" Margaret ran over to where Mrs. Rogers was waiting. "I help my mother, so I know what to do."

Margaret thought it was more fun to help someone else than to do the same thing at her own house.

The two of them walked around the end of the house toward the apple tree and the stone fence across one end of the garden. There were rows of vegetables. Margaret saw carrots, green beans, tomatoes, beets and chard. Red zinnias and blue bachelor buttons grew along one end.

Mrs. Rogers named the flowers as she pointed to the different kinds.

"Those are marigolds." She was pointing to the yellow and orange puff ball flowers with fern-like leaves that encircled the garden. They have a smell that animals don't like, so it helps keep some of them out of there and stops them from helping themselves to my vegetables." Hollyhocks leaned against the stone wall and pumpkin vines trailed off the edge of the wall toward the apple tree.

"Look here," said Mrs. Rogers as she pulled back some large prickly leaves. "These pumpkins are getting big. I'll have to make sure to carry enough water from the lake to keep them growing large."

Margaret looked at the pumpkin vines and could see a few green globes about the size of softballs. "They need to grow a lot more before they're ready for pies. Maybe we could use one for a jack-o-lantern for you this Halloween."

"That would be really fun!" Margaret replied. "I'll help carry water to the pumpkins and other vegetables."

"I hope we don't get an early frost this year. I'm planning to can some tomatoes next week", Mrs. Rogers told Margaret." They are good for spaghetti sauce and soup."

Then she took a pair of scissors out of her apron pocket and cut some white cosmos and red zinnias.

We'll take these in to your mother for a bouquet for your table. Come with me while I put them in a vase with some water. Then you can run these in to your mother, but come back to my place so we can get started on the cookies.

"How pretty," exclaimed Margaret. "Mother will like these."

Mrs. Rogers put the scissors back in her pocket and picked up another log from the woodpile as she went in her back door.

Margaret came back just as she was opening the stove lid to add the new log to the fire.

"This will keep the temperature just right for baking cookies," declared Mrs. Rogers.

"Mother said she loved the flowers and to tell you thank you. So I did," Margaret told Mrs. Rogers.

"She's very welcome," Mrs. Rogers replied. "This kitchen is almost too hot to work in today but we need heat to bake cookies."

Margaret saw four loaves of fresh bread cooling on the kitchen table. She knew that Mrs. Rogers had been up early to do that.

There was a big bowl sitting on the kitchen table next to the loaves of bread. There was also a big wooden spoon and some measuring cups, a flour sifter, some baking pans and a spatula.

"We're going to make molasses cookies, Margaret. It's a recipe that my mother used to make when I was a little girl." She got a small bench out of the back hallway for Margaret to stand on and tied a washed cotton flour sack high up under her arms. That will work as an apron to keep your clothes clean while we cook.

That really isn't necessary, thought Margaret. After all, she'd been wearing the same jeans and blouse for three days, now. She let Mrs. Rogers tie the cloth around her and she climbed up on the bench so she could see into the bowl. There was brown sugar and shortening and molasses already there.

"Can you mix those ingredients to make a smooth batter?"

"I sure can."

Margaret took the big spoon and began to stir. The warm room had made the molasses thin and runny, so it was an easy job. She stirred as Mrs. Rogers added flour, baking soda and spices with the sifter. Now the dough got stiffer and hard to stir but  Margaret kept working it until it was all smooth and light brown.

"You did a very good job with that. Now comes the fun and messy part. Make sure your hands are clean." She showed Margaret where the wash pan was in the sink, next to the cistern pump. Margaret grabbed the big bar of soap and held it under the water flow as Mrs. Rogers slowly pumped the handle. She rubbed the soap, put it back in the dish and then rubbed her hands together to make bubbles. She rinsed them in the wash pan and wiped them dry on her flour sack apron.

"There, I'm ready to make cookies," beamed Margaret.

"Now take a big pinch of dough about this big," said Mrs. Rogers. "Roll it between your hands to make a ball, dip it in this saucer of sugar and then lay it on the baking pan. Try to make the balls all the same size so they'll bake evenly and put them far enough apart so they don't run into each other. Like this." Mrs. Rogers took a few dough balls off the pan and put them on another. "That looks good. Now the last step before we bake them is to put two drops of water on each cookie. That will make them have crackled tops. I'll put these in the oven while you roll some more to fill this pan."

Soon the room was filled with the wonderful smell of molasses and spice and Mrs. Rogers took the first pan out of the oven. Margaret's mouth watered. We'll let them cool a bit before we taste them. While the last pan was baking, Mrs. Rogers began to wash up the things they had used to make the cookies. Margaret moved her bench over to the sink to help.

They finished washing and drying the baking things.

"Now it's time to sample our work." Mrs. Rogers set out two cups, each half filled with milk and poured tea from a teapot into them. She put some of the fresh cookies on a plate and they enjoyed the tea party. "We're a great team, don't you think, Margaret?"

Margaret had her mouth full of the warm molasses cookie so that she could only nod her head in agreement.

Mrs. Rogers refilled the plate of cookies. "Let's take some of these over to your mother." They walked over to the other side of the house.

"We brought you something," Margaret called from the doorway."

"Oh, thank you. First flowers and now cookies. They smell delicious! I still have to put things away in the closets and the chests upstairs and then maybe I will be able to get back to my knitting this evening."

"They are delicious," Margaret assured her mother.

You can enjoy molasses cookies also, by using this:

MRS. ROGERS' MOLASSES COOKIES

Mix together thoroughly......

3/4 cup soft margarine (1 and 1/2 sticks)
1 cup brown sugar (lightly packed)
1 egg
1/4 cup molasses

Sift together and stir in......

2 1/4 cups flour
2 teaspoons baking soda
1/2 teaspoon ground cloves
1 teaspoon cinnamon
1 teaspoon ginger

(If the dough is too soft to make into balls, put it in the refrigerator for 15 to 20 minutes.)
 Roll into balls the size of large walnuts. Dip tops in sugar. Place, sugared side up, 3 inches apart on greased baking sheet. Sprinkle each cookie with 2 drops of water to produce a crackled surface. Bake just until set but not hard at 375 degrees for 10 to 12 minutes. Makes about 4 dozen cookies.

Thomas and his father came in from outside.

"Would you like to go up in the tower, Margaret?"

"Oh, yes," Margaret loudly sang out. I've been waiting to do that."

"Make sure your shoestrings are tied," advised Thomas. "You don't want to trip on them and be sure to use the handrail. Just take it easy, one step at a time."

Margaret did as she was told, and step by step she climbed the ninety-six steps until she found herself at the top. It made her dizzy to look down through the lacy iron steps and landings.

Father led the way and Thomas brought up the rear, just in case Margaret slipped or needed help. Up they went, past the baffle that kept wind from gusting and blowing out the light and up the ladder to the lantern room at the top.

"This is it!" announced Thomas. "This is our Third Order Fresnel lens and the reason for Seul Choix Point Light Station. Look at that view!" As they looked toward the southeast, a clear blue sky and turquoise water showed land on the horizon. You can see Beaver Island today and smoke streaming from a ship out in the shipping channel. That ship is on its way back from Chicago and is carrying a load of coal for Marquette. Then it will pick up another load of iron ore in Marquette before going back to Chicago."

A third order Fresnel (Pronounced fren-el) lens was 5 ft. high by 3 ft. wide. It was made of separate, hand polished prisms, fitted into a metal frame. The prisms gathered the light or flame into a concentrated beam which made a brighter light to be visible for greater distances. The light at Seul Choix was a third order light.

There were other orders of Fresnel lenses and they varied in size. A first order lens was 10 ft. high and 6 ft. wide and a sixth order lens was 8 ft. high and 3 ft. wide.

The Fresnel lens was invented by the French physicist, Augustin Fresnel, in 1822. The lenses were manufactured in Paris, shipped to the United States and other countries and reassembled inside the lantern rooms at the lighthouses.

"How do you know that?" asked Margaret, curiously.

"Captain Rogers showed me the log book just before we came up here."

"The mirrors need to be polished today and I brought along the cloths and some vinegar water to do the job. It's a job that must be done every day because the kerosene makes greasy smoke on the mirrors and the windows", explained Father.

While Thomas and his father cleaned and polished the mirrors and windows, Margaret watched a ship heading east. She waved at it but could see no response. She was too small to be noticed. When the ship was just a spot on the eastern horizon, Thomas said, "Seen enough? Would you like to see the horses, now?" They all made their way back down the stairway to the bottom of the tower stairs. Margaret and Thomas went out to the yard while Father stayed at the desk in the office to log in the ship which had just passed Seul Choix, heading for Sault Saint Marie and the locks.

Outside Thomas and Margaret walked over to the fenced-in barnyard. Margaret bent down and pulled a handful of long grass and held it out toward one of the horses that was nearby. The horse walked up to her outstretched hand, grabbed the grass with big teeth and began chewing. After a few more handsful of grass Margaret noticed some children near the shore catching minnows.

"Hello," Margaret called out to them.

"Hello," came a reply.

She walked toward a girl about her age who was wearing a dress and the skirt was tucked into the legs of her underpants.

"Hi, what's your name?" inquired the girl.

"It's Margaret," Margaret replied shyly. "We just moved here from Beaver Island --- out there," as she pointed out into Lake Michigan.

"My name is Anna," offered the new girl.

Margaret noticed her bare feet, dark skin and straight black hair. The skirt of her dress was wet to the waist.

"Want to catch minnows?" asked Anna.

"OK, But I have to take off my shoes and socks."

Anna waited for her, with minnow pail in her hand, while Margaret put her shoes and socks on a rock and rolled up the legs of her overalls above her knees.

The two girls joined some other children in the water to chase schools of minnows into the bucket. When Anna said that her bucket was full and she had to go back home, Margaret felt sad. She'd just met a friend and they had to part, too soon.

"School starts on Tuesday", announced Anna. "What grade are you in?"

"I'll start third grade this year", answered Margaret.

"So will I," replied Anna. "Good. We'll be in the same class. Everyone is in the same room," called Anna as they parted at the gate to the lighthouse. Anna started down the dirt path toward her home in the fishing village which was on the other side of the schoolhouse. Margaret watched her go and they waved to each other just before Anna disappeared into the woods.

Margaret went back to the shore to retrieve her shoes and ran up the steps to her house to tell her mother about the new friend she had just met.

On Monday, which was Labor Day, and the last official day of summer, Mrs. Rogers had Margaret's mother help her set up tables in the yard and families from the fishing village came to the lighthouse bringing baskets with dishes of food to share for the annual neighborhood picnic. It had been assigned duty at the lighthouse for many years and Mrs. Rogers was happy to carry on the tradition.

All the women fixed their best dishes of food to share with the group as men took the day off from their work and children celebrated end of summer. Older children organized games of tag and foot races for the younger ones and then everyone joined in a lively baseball game to end the day.

Earlier, Mrs. Rogers had gone down in the basement to find the hand-cranked ice cream maker and had sent

Thomas out to the ice house to retrieve whatever ice had survived the summer heat in its layers of sawdust insulation. By searching thoroughly, he had discovered nearly a wash tub full of small pieces.

"That should be just about enough ice," Mrs. Rogers declared as she looked in the tub.

"This morning, I mixed up a double batch of vanilla ice cream and it will take all of you to turn the crank long enough to freeze the ice cream."

Mrs. Rogers poured the ice cream mixture into the center metal cylinder, clamped on the lid, attached the bracket and handle and then packed the space between the cylinder and wooden bucket with pieces of ice and rock salt, until she could fit no more.

"As the ice melts, let the salt water run out of the bucket and pack more ice and salt into the space," advised Mrs. Rogers.

Thomas and his friends took turns turning the crank of the ice cream maker for a long time, until finally the mixture got so stiff the handle would crank no more.

"I think it's done," called Thomas to Mrs. Rogers who was over by the table that still held several cakes. She took a pan and knife and went over to the ice cream maker. She unlatched the crank from the top and pulled out the paddles, thickly covered with semi-frozen ice cream. Using her knife, she scraped all the excess back into the container, clamped the lid on tightly, dumped the ice water out and packed more ice and salt around the cylinder to let it set up. She let the younger children scrape the paddles clean with their spoons before she took them in the house to wash them.

When she returned, the ice cream was solid enough to be dished up. Everyone lined up with their plates to have a piece of cake and a spoonful of the sweet, cold ice cream. A delicious treat to end a wonderful day.

On Tuesday Margaret put on the new plaid dress that her mother had made for her before they left Beaver Island. She and Thomas ate their usual bowls of oatmeal and they each took a peanutbutter and jam sandwich, that mother fixed for them, in a tin lunch pail. They headed off down the lane toward the one room school. That building also served as the church and a meeting house for the peninsula. Margaret felt a mixture of excitement and anticipation as well as a little fear. This was another "first" in her young life. Her mother had been their teacher, at home, until now.

At school, Margaret discovered many children from the area. She noticed Anna standing with a small group in the schoolyard.

Anna came over to her and they said "hi" to each other and then she began to feel more at ease. The teacher, Miss Winters, came to the door and rang the hand bell. She was a friendly looking young woman dressed in a white blouse and long, black skirt. Her hair was piled up on top of her head and tied with a black ribbon. The bell announced that school was officially open for the day.

"Good morning to each of you," she greeted them as they filed through the doorway. "Come in and take a seat, according to your grade. All eighth graders, sit at the larger desks at the back of the room. Then seventh, sixth, fifth, fourth, third, second and first graders at the front of the room at the smaller desks right in front of my desk. Today, we will get to know one another and get organized."

There were more third and fourth graders so some of them had to take the larger desks that were too big and their feet didn't touch the floor.

"At the back of the room there is a row of hooks for you to hang your coats. Please put your lunch pails on the shelf, above your coat," Miss Winters told the children. "Then come back to your desks."

The bigger ones helped the smaller ones put their belongings in the proper places. In the middle of the room, near the coat hooks, there was a big round wood stove. Today was warm, so there was no fire in the stove,

That first day of school was fun for Margaret and she felt proud when it was her turn to read the first two paragraphs in the FOURTH MCGUFFY READER. She read smoothly and clearly except when she came to the unfamiliar word, "awkward". She didn't recognize that word, until Miss Winters pronounced it for her.

Miss Winters worked one-on-one with all the new students that first day, until she came to know how well they read and understood. After that, she assigned one of the older students to tutor each of the younger ones. That way she could have everyone working on lessons as she taught new lessons to each class.

Margaret and Thomas proved to be very good students. Their mother's home teaching at the Beaver Island Lighthouse had put them at the top of their classes. Soon Margaret was tutoring first graders and Thomas was so advanced that he became Miss Winter's best assistant.

William, one of the boys from the fishing village often rode his old horse, Mike, to school. When the horse reached the school, William jumped off, slapped Old Mike on the flank and the horse turned around and went back down the trail to home. That meant that William had to walk home after school. He hadn't trained Old Mike to come to school to let him ride home.

The school year progressed and soon it was Halloween. Margaret got the pumpkin from Mrs. Roger's garden that she had watered all summer with water from the lake. It had grown too big for Margaret to pick up so Thomas and Mrs. Rogers helped put it in the old wagon so they could take it to school and carve it for a jack-o-lantern.

Thomas and Jim, a boy from the fishing village, had become good friends. Jim was often needed to help on the fish boats or with packing fish into crates to ship by railway to Chicago. It was usually his job to drive the horses and wagon to the train station with barrels full of salted or iced fish. Lately, he often invited Thomas to go along. All of the families in the village worked very hard at their businesses and Thomas admired the work they did so he was always happy when Jim asked him to help out.

Sometimes Jim came down to the lighthouse to talk with Thomas and the assistants who slept in the loft over the horse stable. The boys caught minnows under the dock to use for bait on fishing trips out of the harbor or followed the young assistants as they went about their duties in the boat house or the fog signal building.

The waters around Seul Choix Point were abundant with whitefish and trout and that was why the fishing village had been here long before the lighthouse. All the rocky shoals made ideal habitat for fish. The shoals were also what made this area so dangerous for ships. From the surface of the water, just a few rocks could be seen. From the top of the lighthouse, a few more could be seen. Unsuspecting ships didn't know how dangerous this area could be and before the lighthouse was built, several got hung up and ripped open on the rocks near Seul Choix. Even now, with the lighthouse here, a storm could blow a ship off course and put it in danger.

One night after Margaret was in bed, Mother had read another chapter in the latest book, turned out the lamp and had gone downstairs to her knitting.

Thomas and Jim were sitting on the porch talking about the bear claw marks they'd seen on a tree along the wagon trail into Whitedale that day. As they talked, their imaginations took over.

"Wouldn't it be fun to scare your sister?" Jim blurted out.

Now, sometimes even the best of brothers agrees to the worst of mischief when a good friend is involved. Next thing they knew, they had shinnied up the drain spout that ran down into the basement cistern from the eaves. They quietly slid across the roof over to Margaret's bedroom window. While Jim scratched at the screen with a stick, Thomas made low growling noises.

Margaret awoke, screamed loudly and ran down the stairs.

"A bear is trying to get in my window!"

Mother suspected that it wasn't a bear but went upstairs to Margaret's room just in time to see, in the faint light from the fog signal building, the two boys scrambling across the roof and sliding down the drain pipe. She went back downstairs and outdoors to see Thomas and Jim walking toward the fog signal building. When she confronted them about the mischief, they confessed and of course, promised never to do that again.

Margaret's father was up in the light tower, on watch when heavy fog rolled in off the water. He had first suspected bad weather just before sunset. He had his powerful binoculars trained on the southeast, toward Beaver Island. The sky seemed to melt into the water so he couldn't tell where the horizon was. There was no wind this evening and he could no longer see the faint light at White Shoal.

He set the binoculars on the sill of the light tower and checked the reservoir at the base of the Fresnel lens. There was plenty of fuel for the next few hours, so he lit it using the matches from the brass tinderbox which was clipped to his belt. Then he opened the hatch on the floor and climbed down the ladder. He reached up to close the hatch before he reached the next one. He was always careful to keep those closed when the light was lit because any sudden gust of wind could blow out the flame. Ships depended on this lighthouse to steer them away from the rocks.

After the second hatch he was on the lacy iron circular stairway. Faint light from the windows and the office below let him see well enough. He held the handrail, kept to the outside of the steps, the wide end, and made his way down. He took a lantern from the office and went out to awaken the young assistants who were bunking there. They slept when they could and it was usually a light sleep because they knew they were always "on call".

Almost immediately, two young sailors dressed in bellbottom blue jeans and chambray shirts followed him out to the fog signal building. They got the fire going in the boiler and about twenty minutes later the engine had built up enough steam pressure to blast the sound from the foghorns out into the night.

With the first "OOUU-WAAA" blast from the foghorns, Margaret jumped up to look out her bedroom window. All she could see through the mist was a faint light in the fog signal building and heard her father and the assistants giving and taking orders as they carried out their duties. Then she saw Thomas standing in the doorway taking in all the excitement. She wasn't frightened because she was used to the horn on Beaver Island. That one was farther away from the house so it wasn't so loud but the sound was comforting so she went back to sleep.

Thomas had heard the commotion while he was at the kitchen table doing his homework. He went out to the fog signal building and now was sitting on the short spiral stairway in the middle of the building watching everything, memorizing the procedure so he would be able to help, if ever needed.

He had looked at the charts and knew that this area of Lake Michigan was littered with skeletons of ships that hadn't been warned, in the days before Seul Choix Lighthouse was built. There were ships out on the lake now. There was always heavy traffic in this area from May until late December. Thomas' father looked around and saw that everything was under control and running smoothly so he went back to finish his watch in the tower.

On one of the last warm Saturdays after school had begun Jim came around the point in one of his family's rowboats. He had another boy from the fishing village with him.

"We're going out to Gull Island to look for eggs. Want to come along?" Jim called to Thomas as they pulled the boat alongside the dock.

Thomas was out by the barn, fixing the latch on the fence around the horse yard. "Yea, sure. I just have to put these tools away. I don't have anymore chores, today."

Gull Island was a small island, just visible on the horizon and it was a trip that the other boys had made many times, so no one bothered to tell anyone where they were going. Besides, they would be back long before dark.

The day was perfect for a trip out to the island. Soft breezes and gentle swells made rowing easy. They took turns at the oars and soon they were pulling the boat up on shore.

No one lived on Gull Island except for the gulls. It was small and strewn with huge rocks, some scrub brush and a few wind-twisted, gnarly spruce trees. They had the whole island to themselves to explore. But first, they gathered around a big, flat rock to use as a table for their stolen picnic. Jim had brought a loaf of bread that had been cooling on his kitchen table. There were so many kids at his house that his mother made about a dozen loaves at a time and no one would miss one loaf today. Ed had managed to get a small chunk of cheese from the cupboard at his house. They tore the bread into pieces and Ed used his pocketknife to cut slices of cheese. Clear water from the lake satisfied their thirst.

"I see some raspberries over there", called Ed and they all walked over to have some dessert. There were also blueberries growing nearly everywhere.

After almost an hour of walking and picking and eating berries, they realized that they hadn't seen one gull nest.

"All the gull eggs must have hatched and the nests have been abandoned for a while", Thomas said. "After all, it's pretty late in the season.

Suddenly he noticed that the sky had turned dark and threatening in the northeast and winds had begun to blow the trees around and sent them bouncing and bobbing on their trunks. "We had better head back to the point."

When they returned to the beached boat they all realized that it was too late to get out on the lake in their small boat. Angry waves were rolling over it and the lake was a wild, splashing gray mass. Rain began to pound them so they pulled the boat up by some scrubby cedar trees and turned it upside down to give them some protection.

The storm raged all night and the next day as the boys huddled under the upturned boat. On the third day the rain let up while strong winds continued to blow.

"Maybe we will never be able to go back home", Thomas began to worry. It wasn't like him to go somewhere without telling some of his family. Even Jim and Ed who were less watched-over than Thomas, expressed concern that they might be missed.

The bread and cheese were long gone and they had picked all the berries on the protected side of the island. Even lake water was full of sand when they cupped their hands in it for a drink. This wasn't the adventure they had imagined when they left the dock at Seul Choix. It had been a very long time since then. Today they decided to leave a record of their trip here in case they didn't make it back home.

The boys discussed this and located a good-sized rock that they could use for a message. Using Ed's pocketknife, they took turns scratching and carving their names and a date on the rock. And still the storm raged on for nearly a week. Thomas knew that his mother and father and Margaret were worried about him and he was sorry for leaving without telling anyone. The boys had been able to see the lighthouse flashing and beckoning them home from the second night but no one knew they were out here and their small boat would never make it through the deep, choppy waves to safety.

As quickly as the storm had come up, it blew itself out. The next morning they awoke to clear blue skies and calm water. Three dirty, hungry, mosquito-bitten young men turned their boat over, located the oars and pushed it out to row back home.

Thomas' father was up in the light tower scanning the horizon, when he spotted the boat, just a dot on the horizon. His trained eyes followed the dot as it neared the point and into the harbor. Word spread throughout the point that the boys were found and were returning.

Some people from the fishing village and everyone from the lighthouse were at the dock to welcome them back. Thomas spotted his mother at the front of the crowd. Her anger and frustration had been replaced with relief as she hugged her filthy, bedraggled son.

After their adventure and safe return, the three young men became folk heroes in the neighborhood but they never spoke of the rock they had carved and even through some others who went out to Gull Island discovered it, the carved rock remained undisturbed for many, many years.

On New Year's Day, Thomas tested the ice in the harbor and came inside to announce that it was thick enough to begin harvesting. That was a chore that took place during the coldest part of winter and was necessary for the fishing business. They needed the ice to preserve fish for Chicago markets and people at the lighthouse used it in their ice-boxes during summer. It was also the essential ingredient when making ice cream. Men with big saws cut blocks and layered it with sawdust from nearby sawmills, for insulation during the heat of summer. It was stored in wooden icehouses along the shore, sheltered by shade of big trees. If they harvested all winter, the ice would usually last until September when the weather cooled.

Ice harvesting also meant ice-skating! When Margaret heard the discussion about ice, she asked her mother if they could have a skating party on Saturday. Mrs. Rogers was also told about the

skating plans.

Word about the party spread quickly throughout the peninsula and on Saturday afternoon children and adults began gathering on shore, near the lighthouse dock. Soon groups of skaters were gliding across the frozen bay. Someone built a bonfire on the shoreline to help warm frozen toes and fingers. Children never felt cold until the skating was done. Only then did they realize they needed to get warm, while suffering the stings of thawing out.

As the sun began dropping to the west and early darkness closed in, Mrs. Rogers called from the porch, "Come on in, everybody. We've made cocoa and popcorn and we have apples for everyone."

After "good-bye"s and "thank-you"s, everyone left the lighthouse for home while the beacon of the lighthouse lit their way.

Friends and families still gather at Seul Choix each year on Labor Day, with food and entertainment. These days, the crowd is too large to fit into the house, so the food is a pot luck meal, served in the yard and entertainment is usually a talk by a former keeper or a member of his family. There is always maritime music provided by talented former residents and neighbors. And, of course, stories around the campfire.

DEDICATION

This book is dedicated to my husband, Robert and my daughter, Deborah.

Without their hours of patient help and eyesight, this never would have come

to be.

And also in memory of Gail for ideas and encouragement.

ISBN 141200685-6